The Frequency of Money

Dr. Of Money
Ameca Cooley

Table Of Contents

Chapter 1

Introduction to The Frequency of Money

Setting the Tone: Money as More Than Currency

Money, in its physical form, is a tangible representation of value and exchange. Yet, as we embark on a journey to explore the frequencies of money, we're invited to step beyond its mere material presence. The first chapter of this book aims to set the tone by unraveling the idea that money is more than just currency. It's a complex web of energies, vibrations, and frequencies that weave through our lives.

In a world often defined by the pursuit of financial gain, we tend to overlook the subtle currents of energy that flow beneath the surface. From ancient cultures to modern financial systems, money has always held a power that goes beyond its face value. It influences our decisions, shapes our aspirations, and even impacts the societal structures we inhabit. However, what if money's influence transcends the physical and ventures into the realm of the unseen?

In some metaphysical circles, the concept of money being a vibration, frequency, or energy is not a new one. Many of these teachings train students to recognize money as a living force that must be harnessed, managed, and directed in order to manifest abundance. This idea put forth by the ancient metaphysical masters takes root in the idea that money is a channel of communication between our physical reality and the greater intelligence. They believed that one's vibrational balance must be aligned with the energy of money.

The Frequency of Money

At its core, this idea is rooted in the use of specific words, visualizations, and affirmations to invoke a divine energy to incite change and alchemy in our material world. Some teachings speak to the power of cultivating a sense of gratitude, or even joy, for money itself, as a way to eradicate any feelings of shame or dread. This can have a powerful effect in improving a person's relationship with money, helping them to eradicate any self-defeating beliefs that may be blocking them from reaching their goals.

Other teachings encourage the use of words that emphasize the positive outcome that you're going to get from taking action. For example, rather than saying, "I don't want to go into debt" or "I'll never make enough money", you could instead say something like "I'm going to make smart financial decisions that lead to economic

The Unseen World of Vibrations and Frequencies

Every object, thought, and emotion carries its own unique vibrational frequency. While we may not perceive these frequencies through our ordinary senses, they are present all around us, shaping our experiences and interactions. From the gentle hum of the universe to the intricate symphonies of atoms, vibrations are the threads that connect the fabric of existence.

In this context, the concept of money takes on a new dimension. Imagine the resonance of a crisp banknote as it exchanges hands, the subtle vibrations of coins cascading into a jar, or the rustling of bills in a wallet. These sounds are not merely auditory; they are energetic signatures that carry the essence of money's movement. Just as musical notes come together to create harmonies, money's frequencies intermingle to shape our financial reality.

As we delve deeper into the frequencies of money, we'll explore the mesmerizing dance between economics, psychology, and metaphysics. We'll uncover the harmony between wealth and well-being, and we'll investigate the ways in which our personal frequencies influence the flow of abundance in our lives. The chapters that follow will unveil the hidden melodies within coins and bills, decipher the allegorical wisdom within ancient scriptures, and provide practical tools to attune ourselves to the frequency of prosperity.

This book is an invitation to explore a world where money is not just a means of transaction, but a force that resonates through our thoughts, actions, and intentions. Through these pages, we'll embark on a transformative journey, one that transcends the physical realm and tunes into the frequencies that shape the symphony of wealth in our lives. Let us begin our exploration of the harmonizing vibrations that underlie the dance of prosperity.

Money has its own unique frequency, an almost music-like composition. Every coin and bill has its own unique sound and vibration, akin to a string on a violin or a bell struck by a mallet. As with instruments, these vibrations fluctuate and combine to form an ever-changing melody, reflecting the ever-shifting dynamics of the economy.

As human beings, we are energy entities too. We likewise vibrate and resonate with different frequencies based on

Money's Movement: The Velocity of Prosperity

Understanding the Velocity of Money

In the world of finance, money's journey is not a solitary once It's a dynamic movement that breathes life into economies and influences the way we navigate our financial landscapes. Chapter 2 delves into the concept of money's velocity, an essential facet of the financial realm that goes beyond the mere exchange of bills and coins.

At its core, the velocity of money refers to the speed at which money circulates within an economy. It's a measure of how often a unit of currency changes hands in a given period. Just as the currents of a river shape the landscape it passes through, the velocity of money shapes economic dynamics. The more frequently money changes hands, the more transactions occur, leading to increased economic activity and growth.

The need for increased currency printing.

The velocity of money is heavily dependent on the behavior and preferences of consumers. Apart from the rate at which consumers purchase goods and services, consumer mindset and sentiment also impact the velocity of money. For example, if people are rationally confident in the economy, they will feel more comfortable spending, which in turn will cause money to circulate more quickly. The same is true when people are skeptical and afraid of taking on debt, as fewer people will make purchases.

The rate of circulation of a currency is not only influenced by consumer behavior; the availability and printing of currency also plays an important role. When a certain currency is printed more frequently or in larger denominations, the velocity of money will be higher, as it will cushion the process of exchanging goods and services. On the other hand, when the same currency is printed too little, it can cause a slowdown in money's movement. In this case, people

How Money's Movement Impacts Economies and Individuals

The movement of money sets the rhythm of economic activity, influencing everything from consumer spending to business investments. When money flows swiftly, it invigorates industries, generates jobs, and fosters innovation. On the other hand, a sluggish circulation can lead to stagnation and reduced opportunities.

At the individual level, understanding the velocity of money offers insights into personal financial management. The faster money circulates in your life, whether through investments, spending, or entrepreneurial endeavors, the greater the potential for growth and accumulation. This chapter examines how aligning your financial decisions with the concept of money's velocity can help you harness its energetic currents to your advantage.

Moreover, the velocity of money reveals a connection to the frequencies discussed in the previous chapter. Just as vibrations and frequencies resonate within every monetary transaction, the velocity at which these transactions occur amplifies the impact of these energies. Whether through the rustling of cash, the jingling of coins, or the subtle hum of digital transactions, money's movement is intricately linked to its vibrational nature.

As we explore the velocity of money, we'll unveil its role in economic cycles, delve into historical examples of how changes in velocity have shaped societies, and examine its correlation with personal financial growth. Through this exploration, we'll uncover the hidden harmonies that arise when money's velocity aligns with its vibrational essence. By the end of this chapter, you'll have a deeper understanding of how the movement of money orchestrates a symphony of prosperity on both macroeconomic and individual levels.

How money's movement plays a critical role in influencing a wide range of economic activities, ranging from consumer spending to investments made by businesses. When money is circulating rapidly, it can be seen as a symbol of healthy economic activity, as it can stimulate industries, create jobs and facilitate innovation. Alternatively, a lagging circulation of money can lead to stagnation and diminishing opportunities.

At an individual level, understanding the velocity of money can be very beneficial for personal fiscal management. By insuring that your finances are kept in perpetual motion – through investment, expenditure and entrepreneurial activities – you maximize your potential for profitability and accumulation.

In this chapter, we will focus on how to take advantage of money's velocity, by exploring the correlation it has with economic cycles, providing historical perspectives on how shifts in velocity have affected societies, and demonstrating how it is linked to personal financial growth.

Understanding the complexities of money's velocity unveils how it resonates and vibrates within each transaction. We will be examining how the sound of cash, coins or digital diversions echoes through the financial system. Which leads us to the conclusion that money's frequencies and its vibrational nature are inextricably linked with one another, as one cannot exist without the other.

In conclusion, by delving into the depths of money's velocity, we will uncover its ability to generate symmetries and create harmony both within economic systems and individual financial aspects. By the time you have completed this chapter, you will be armed with relevant information about how the velocity of money impacts both macroeconomics and the individual.

Chapter 3

The Audible Riches: Rustling and Rattling Frequencies

The Uniqueness of Sound in Money's World

In the symphony of life, money contributes a distinct note of its own unique frequency that resonates through our experiences. Chapter 3 delves into the world of auditory wealth, exploring how the sounds of money, the rustling of paper bills and the clinking of coins create a sensory experience that transcends the material realm.

While our eyes may be the primary senses through which we engage with currency, sound plays an equally vital role. The gentle rustling of paper bills as they're counted or exchanged carries a tactile energy that's inseparable from the concept of value. Likewise, the sharp, resonant tones of coins clashing together conjure images of abundance and prosperity. These sounds are not merely utilitarian; they're carriers of the essence of money's movement.

The Uniqueness of Sound in Money's World in its melodic embrace.

In a sense, the sounds of money reflect the ideas we have about it. For some, the gentle rustling of money may evoke feelings of security and comfort; for others, the jangly music of multiple pieces of loose change may conjure up a sense of freedom and adventure. Regardless of one's individual interpretation, sound and money have a symbiotic relationship.

Throughout the ages, the relationship between sound and money has evolved in various ways, encompassing the realms of music, finance, and technology.

In summary, the relationship between sound and money has undergone continuous evolution, shaped by technological advancements, changes in consumer behavior, and innovative business models. As we move forward, it's likely that new technologies and trends will continue to redefine how sound is monetized in the broader context of the entertainment and creative industries.

Controlled by economic forces and political influence.

In the ancient world, sound had a generally positive reputation as it was seen as a representation of royalty, power, and leadership. Kings and queens of Egypt and Babylon often used sound for communication, celebration, and entertainment, such as music, speeches, and poetry readings. Kings and queens also understood the power of sound. They could create and maintain their standing in society by controlling music, orchestras, and singing. These rituals were also used to influence and consolidate political power. The controlled use of sound was a strategic tool in shaping perceptions, reinforcing authority, and fostering a sense of unity among the people.

1. Ceremonial and Ritualistic Influence:

Coronation Ceremonies: The use of sound in coronation ceremonies was a powerful means of legitimizing rulership. The grandeur of music, speeches, and poetry readings during such events conveyed a sense of divine approval and authority.

2. Symbolism of Sound:

Royal Orchestras and Music: Kings and queens employed musicians and orchestras as symbols of wealth, sophistication, and cultural refinement. The patronage of the arts, including music, served to enhance the ruler's image.

3. Communication and Control:

Speeches and Proclamations: Leaders used sound to convey messages and proclamations. Speeches were an essential means of addressing the populace, and the delivery, tone, and rhetoric were carefully crafted to exert influence and maintain control.

4. Social Unity and Identity:

Music as a Unifying Force: Music, as a communal activity, was harnessed to create a shared cultural identity. Certain melodies or compositions could evoke a sense of patriotism and loyalty among the population.

5. Propaganda and Psychological Warfare:

Poetry and Verses: Poetry readings and recitations were often used to convey narratives that reinforced the ruler's authority or conveyed specific messages. These poetic expressions could be a form of early propaganda.

6. Cultural Engineering:

Control over Artistic Expression: Kings and queens, as patrons of the arts, had the power to shape cultural norms and values. They could influence the themes and messages conveyed through artistic endeavors, reinforcing the desired social order.

7. Intimidation and Display of Power:

Military Parades and Drums: The sound of drums and military parades were not only symbols of military might but also tools of psychological warfare. The rhythmic beats and organized marches could instill fear in potential adversaries and showcase the ruler's strength.

8. Control over Rituals:

Religious Ceremonies: In societies where rulers held both political and religious authority, sound played a crucial role in religious ceremonies. Rulers often controlled or influenced these rituals, reinforcing their divine connection and authority.

9. Perpetuation of Hierarchies:

Control of Musical Talents: By controlling access to skilled musicians, rulers could ensure that the cultural elite aligned with their interests. This control over artistic talents helped perpetuate existing social hierarchies.

In essence, the relationship between sound and power in the ancient world was intricate. Sound was not only a form of artistic expression and entertainment but a tool that rulers strategically wielded to maintain political dominance, shape societal norms, and cultivate a sense of collective identity. The positive reputation of sound was intricately tied to its use as a means of expressing and reinforcing authority.

The most ancient examples of money and sound are coins. Coins were often struck with specific designs in order to signify their worth, as well as to differentiate them from counterfeit coins. Over time, many coins were minted with embossed images that acted as visual reminders of the value of the money. Even more impressive, in some cultures, coins were made with specific shapes and weights in order to facilitate payment. In Greco-Roman literature, coins were even given human-like

Investigating the Frequencies of Paper Bills and Coins

In our exploration of money's frequencies, it's fascinating to consider the specific vibrational signatures that accompany different forms of currency. Paper bills, for example, have a characteristic rustling sound with frequencies typically ranging from 200 Hz to 1000 Hz. This range is reminiscent of the delicate hum of nature, a reminder that even in the midst of commerce, there's an underlying connection to the natural world.

Coins, with their metallic composition, produce higher-pitched sounds. The clinking frequencies of coins often fall between 1000 Hz and 5000 Hz, creating a melody that's both energetic and uplifting. Just as each musical instrument contributes a unique timbre to an orchestra, the various denominations and metals of coins create a rich tapestry of tones that underscore the essence of financial transactions.

This chapter not only examines the science behind these auditory frequencies but also delves into the psychological impact of money's sounds. How does the rustling of bills affect our perception of wealth? What emotions do the clinking coins evoke? By uncovering the layers of meaning embedded in these frequencies, we gain insights into the intricate ways in which our senses shape our financial experiences.

As we explore the rustling and rattling frequencies of money, we'll uncover the role they play in shaping our perceptions, influencing our behaviors, and deepening our connection to the concept of prosperity. The sounds of money are more than auditory cues. They're harmonious threads that weave through the tapestry of our financial lives, enhancing the vibrational symphony of wealth and abundance.

The exploration of the frequencies associated with paper bills and coins adds an interesting dimension to our understanding of the sensory aspects of money. Here's a breakdown of the key points mentioned:

1. Characteristics of Paper Bills:

Frequency Range: The rustling sound of paper bills is described to have frequencies ranging from 200 Hz to 1000 Hz.

Nature Connection: The author draws a poetic connection between the rustling of paper bills and the delicate hum of nature. This metaphor suggests a deeper, almost organic link between commerce and the natural world.

2. Characteristics of Coins:

Frequency Range: Coins, being metallic, produce higher-pitched sounds, typically falling in the range of 1000 Hz to 5000 Hz.

Energetic Melody: The clinking frequencies of coins are characterized as creating a melody that is both energetic and uplifting. This description highlights the dynamic and positive qualities associated with the sound of coins.

3. Psychological Impact:

Perception of Wealth: The chapter hints at exploring how the sound of rustling bills may impact our perception of wealth. The auditory experience of handling money could potentially influence our subconscious associations with affluence and financial well-being.

Emotional Response: Similarly, the emotional response to the clinking sound of coins is suggested to be an area of investigation. Different frequencies may evoke specific emotions, and understanding these connections can provide insights into how we relate to money on a psychological level.

4. Science and Psychology:

Scientific Exploration: The chapter promises to delve into the science behind these auditory frequencies, suggesting a more detailed examination of the physical properties of paper bills and coins that contribute to their characteristic sounds.

Psychological Impact: Beyond the physical aspects, the psychological impact of money's sounds is emphasized. This suggests an exploration of how our senses, particularly hearing, play a role in shaping our financial experiences.

5. Symbolism and Connection:

Metaphorical Language: The use of metaphors, such as "harmonious threads" and a "vibrational symphony of wealth and abundance," adds a layer of symbolism. It suggests that the sounds of money are not just functional but carry a symbolic significance in the broader narrative of prosperity.

6. Interplay of Senses:

Multisensory Experience: The chapter suggests that the sounds of money contribute to a multisensory experience of financial transactions. This implies that our interactions with money involve more than just the visual and tactile; they extend to the auditory realm as well.

In summary, the exploration of money's frequencies not only involves the physical characteristics of paper bills and coins but also delves into the psychological and symbolic dimensions of these sounds. The chapter aims to unravel the layers of meaning embedded in the auditory experience of money, offering insights into how our senses contribute to the complex tapestry of our financial lives.

Chapter 4

Melodic Money: The Rustling Frequencies (200 Hz - 1000 Hz)

Exploring the Frequencies of Paper Currency

In the realm of financial frequencies, the rustling of paper currency offers a melody of its own. Chapter 4 delves into the rhythmic vibrations produced by the movement of paper bills, exploring the spectrum of frequencies that characterize this auditory experience. From the delicate whisper of banknotes being counted to the satisfying shuffle of bills exchanging hands, the rustling frequencies of money form an integral part of the tapestry of wealth.

The frequencies of paper currency, which typically fall within the range of 200 Hz to 1000 Hz, hold a unique space in our perception of value. These vibrations form a bridge between the tactile world of commerce and the realm of sensory experience. Just as a musician's fingers on guitar strings create vibrations that produce notes, the motion of handling paper money generates vibrations that resonate with our senses.

How the Rustling Sound Reflects Money's Energy

The rustling sound of paper currency encapsulates the energetic flow of money's movement. It's more than a mere auditory backdrop, it's a testament to the circulation of wealth, an echo of transactions, and a symbol of prosperity in action. This chapter invites us to explore the symbolism behind the rustling frequencies, considering how they reflect the essence of money's energy.

Just as the rustling of leaves in a forest carries the promise of growth and renewal, the rustling of bills carries the promise of financial exchange and growth. It signifies the movement of resources, the transfer of value, and the continuous dance of economic activity. When we listen to the rustling frequencies, we're tuning into the symphony of abundance that plays out in every transaction.

Furthermore, the rustling frequencies connect us to the tactile nature of money connection that's often overlooked in today's digital world. The act of handling physical currency engages our senses and deepens our connection to the concept of value. The rustling frequencies become a reminder that wealth is not just numbers on a screen; it's a tangible, sensory experience that resonates with the frequencies of life itself.

As we delve into the melodic qualities of the rustling frequencies, we'll explore their role in shaping our perceptions of value, their impact on consumer behavior, and their resonance with ancient practices of wealth exchange. By understanding the vibrational significance of these frequencies, we begin to see money not as a static object, but as a dynamic force that harmonizes with the frequencies of prosperity.

Chapter 5

Melodic Money: The Rustling Frequencies (200 Hz - 1000 Hz)

Exploring the Frequencies of Paper Currency

In this chapter, we embark on a journey to uncover the subtle harmonies that resonate within the rustling frequencies of paper currency. The very act of handling money involves a sensory experience that extends beyond the visual, and these frequencies offer a musical quality to our financial interactions.

How the Rustling Sound Reflects Money's Energy

The rustling sound of paper currency creates a bridge between the tactile reality of commerce and the world of sensory perception. The frequencies, ranging from 200 Hz to 1000 Hz, are a symphony of their own symphony that whispers of transactions, potential, and the movement of wealth. These vibrations become the soundtrack of economic activity, the rhythm of prosperity in motion.

The rustling frequencies mirror the energy of money's circulation. Imagine the sound of bills changing hands rustling, and it represents an exchange of value, a connection between individuals, and a flow of resources. It's a reminder that money is not static; it's alive with the energy of movement, much like a river that flows to nurture the land it touches.

When we explore the rustling frequencies, we enter the world of sensory economics. The touch of paper, the swish of bills, and the sound of transactions all contribute to our perception of value. This chapter invites us to contemplate how these frequencies affect our subconscious understanding of wealth. The auditory experience becomes a part of the story that money tells an ever-present undercurrent that enhances our connection to the physical representation of prosperity.

Furthermore, the rustling sound evokes a sense of anticipation and excitement. Just as the opening notes of a musical piece set the stage for what's to come, the rustling frequencies precede moments of exchange, inviting us to engage in the symphony of economic interactions. The rustling sound is a universal reminder that abundance is not a static concept; it's alive with motion, growth, and change.

As we journey through the rustling frequencies, we'll uncover their role in psychological associations with money, their connection to personal and cultural perceptions of value, and their influence on our financial behaviors. By embracing the melodic nature of money's rustling frequencies, we open ourselves to a deeper understanding of the harmonies that weave through our financial lives.

I challenge you to do what I teach my students to put cash in your wallet and pocket. Take it out to rub it, so you can hear the rustling of the money to produce a vibrational frequency in your hand. Click this link now to subscribe to my YouTube channel to listen to money sounds.

https://youtube.com/@nowinvestmentsinc5217?si=z-UEhb3cT0VMUJbQ

Coin Cadence: The Clanging Frequencies (1000 Hz - 5000 Hz)

Delving into the Vibrations of Coins

In the realm of currency, coins occupy a unique space as carriers of both material and symbolic value. Chapter 5 invites us to explore the world of coin vibrations, delving into the auditory experience of coins clinking together and the energetic significance behind the frequencies they produce.

The Vibrational Chorus of Coins

Coins, with their metallic composition, generate higher-pitched sounds compared to paper currency. These clanging frequencies, ranging from 1000 Hz to 5000 Hz, create a cadence that echoes through transactions and embodies the essence of wealth in its tangible form. Just as different musical instruments contribute their distinct tones to an orchestra, different denominations of coins contribute their own vibrational notes to the financial symphony.

The Symbolism Behind the Higher Frequencies

The higher frequencies of coin clinks carry symbolism that extends beyond the auditory realm. These tones often evoke feelings of excitement, vibrancy, and elevation. When we hear the resonance of coins, we're tapping into an auditory expression of the dynamic movement of wealth. The energetic frequencies of coins reflect their role as tangible representations of value and abundance.

Additionally, the clanging frequencies of coins carry the energy of exchange. As coins are exchanged between individuals, their frequencies create a vibrational bridge that connects people through commerce. This interplay of vibrations embodies the concept of value flowing freely, just as frequencies ripple through the air to create harmonious sound waves.

The chapter not only explores the physics of coin vibrations but also delves into the psychology of their symbolism. What do the higher frequencies evoke in our consciousness? How do these auditory experiences influence our perceptions of wealth and abundance? By unraveling these questions, we gain a deeper understanding of the multi-layered influence of coin cadence on our financial experiences.

As we navigate the terrain of clanging frequencies, we'll uncover their connection to cultural practices, their impact on our emotions, and their resonance with ancient traditions of prosperity. By embracing the vibrational cadence of coins, we begin to resonate with the symphony of wealth, tuning into the frequencies that weave through every exchange and celebration of abundance.

I challenge you to keep a minimum of four quarters in your pocket and let them clang together daily to produce a money frequency in your pocket.

The exploration of higher frequencies associated with the clinking of coins delves into the symbolic, psychological, and even practical aspects of this auditory experience. Here's a breakdown of the key points mentioned:

1. Symbolism of Higher Frequencies:

Feelings of Excitement and Vibrancy: The chapter suggests that the higher frequencies of coin clinks evoke feelings of excitement, vibrancy, and elevation. This implies a positive and dynamic association with the sound of coins, linking it to the energetic movement of wealth.

Representation of Value and Abundance: The energetic frequencies of coins are described as reflections of their role as tangible representations of value and abundance. This symbolism connects the physical presence of coins to broader concepts of prosperity.

2. Energy of Exchange:

Vibrational Bridge: The clanging frequencies of coins are metaphorically presented as creating a vibrational bridge between individuals during exchanges. This imagery suggests that the sound of coins embodies the dynamic flow of value in commercial transactions.

Symbol of Free-Flowing Value: The interplay of vibrations is portrayed as representing the free flow of value, similar to how frequencies ripple through the air to create harmonious sound waves. This concept aligns with the idea of a fluid and interconnected economic exchange.

3. Physics and Psychology:

Physics of Coin Vibrations: The chapter promises an exploration of the physics behind coin vibrations, suggesting a scientific understanding of how coins produce their characteristic higher frequencies.

Psychological Symbolism: Beyond the physical aspects, the chapter indicates a focus on the psychology of the symbolism associated with higher frequencies. This suggests an examination of how our subconscious interprets and responds to the auditory experience of coin clinking.

4. Cultural Practices and Ancient Traditions:

Connection to Cultural Practices: The exploration extends to the connection between clanging frequencies and cultural practices. This implies that the sound of coins is not only a contemporary phenomenon but may have historical and cultural significance.

Resonance with Ancient Traditions: The chapter hints at uncovering the resonance of coin cadence with ancient traditions of prosperity, suggesting a deeper historical context to the auditory experience of coins.

5. Personal Challenge:

Practical Application: The chapter concludes with a personal challenge, encouraging readers to keep quarters in their pockets and let them clang together daily. This practical application implies that actively engaging with the sound of coins is a way to create a personal "money frequency" and potentially influence one's financial mindset.

In summary, the exploration of higher frequencies associated with coins goes beyond the physical characteristics of sound. It delves into the symbolic and psychological dimensions, connects the auditory experience to cultural practices and ancient traditions, and even proposes a practical challenge to engage with the sound of coins for personal enrichment. This multi-faceted approach aims to provide a comprehensive understanding of the role of coin cadence in shaping our perceptions and experiences of wealth.

Chapter 7

The Parable of Prosperity: Matthew 25

Analyzing the Parable of the Talents

In the sacred realm of spiritual texts, certain teachings hold timeless wisdom that transcends boundaries. Chapter 6 takes us on a reflective journey into the Parable of the Talents, a story found in the Gospel of Matthew, to extract profound insights into the realms of investment, stewardship, and multiplication.

Unveiling the Parable of the Talents

In Matthew 25:14-30, we encounter a powerful allegory a master entrusts his servants with different amounts of money (talents) before embarking on a journey. Upon his return, he assesses their stewardship. Two of the servants, who invested their talents and doubled their resources, are commended and rewarded. The third servant, who buried his talent out of fear, is reprimanded.

This parable's implications ripple through the ages, speaking to the heart of financial stewardship. It introduces a universal theme, the delicate dance between risk and reward, and the dynamic interplay of action and inaction. Just as vibrations and frequencies are forces that shape our reality, the actions and decisions we make ripple through our financial journey.

Extracting Wisdom on Investment, Stewardship, and Multiplication

The Parable of the Talents is a microcosm of financial principles that resonate through centuries. It speaks to the significance of investing resources, whether monetary or otherwise, and nurturing them to fruition. The two servants who multiplied their talents demonstrated the concept of responsible investments where measured risks yield substantial rewards.

The third servant, on the other hand, represents a cautionary tale about fear and complacency. Burying his talent symbolizes missed opportunities and the stagnation that comes with resisting growth. His choice echoes the inaction that often accompanies a scarcity mindset, one that resists vibrational alignment with abundance.

By dissecting this parable, we gain insights into the principles that guide wealth accumulation and financial expansion. We uncover the essence of stewardship, our role as caretakers of resources and the pivotal role of action in generating vibrational momentum. Just as frequencies build upon each other to create harmonies, our actions and decisions in the realm of finance compound to shape our financial symphony.

In this chapter, we'll delve into the layers of symbolism within the Parable of the Talents. We'll draw parallels between the parable's messages and the frequency of money discussed earlier in the book. Through this analysis, we'll unearth a treasure trove of wisdom that guides us on a path of enlightened financial stewardship, aligning our actions with the frequencies of prosperity and abundance.

The exploration of higher frequencies associated with the clinking of coins delves into the symbolic, psychological, and even practical aspects of this auditory experience. Here's a breakdown of the key points mentioned:

1. Symbolism of Higher Frequencies:

Feelings of Excitement and Vibrancy: The chapter suggests that the higher frequencies of coin clinks evoke feelings of excitement, vibrancy, and elevation. This implies a positive and dynamic association with the sound of coins, linking it to the energetic movement of wealth.

Representation of Value and Abundance: The energetic frequencies of coins are described as reflections of their role as tangible representations of value and abundance. This symbolism connects the physical presence of coins to broader concepts of prosperity.

2. Energy of Exchange:

Vibrational Bridge: The clanging frequencies of coins are metaphorically presented as creating a vibrational bridge between individuals during exchanges. This imagery suggests that the sound of coins embodies the dynamic flow of value in commercial transactions.

Symbol of Free-Flowing Value: The interplay of vibrations is portrayed as representing the free flow of value, similar to how frequencies ripple through the air to create harmonious sound waves. This concept aligns with the idea of a fluid and interconnected economic exchange.

3. Physics and Psychology:

Physics of Coin Vibrations: The chapter promises an exploration of the physics behind coin vibrations, suggesting a scientific understanding of how coins produce their characteristic higher frequencies.

Psychological Symbolism: Beyond the physical aspects, the chapter indicates a focus on the psychology of the symbolism associated with higher frequencies. This suggests an examination of how our subconscious interprets and responds to the auditory experience of coin clinking.

4. Cultural Practices and Ancient Traditions:

Connection to Cultural Practices: The exploration extends to the connection between clanging frequencies and cultural practices. This implies that the sound of coins is not only a contemporary phenomenon but may have historical and cultural significance.

Resonance with Ancient Traditions: The chapter hints at uncovering the resonance of coin cadence with ancient traditions of prosperity, suggesting a deeper historical context to the auditory experience of coins.

5. Personal Challenge:

Practical Application: The chapter concludes with a personal challenge, encouraging readers to keep quarters in their pockets and let them clang together daily. This practical application implies that actively engaging with the sound of coins is a way to create a personal "money frequency" and potentially influence one's financial mindset.

In summary, the exploration of higher frequencies associated with coins goes beyond the physical characteristics of sound. It delves into the symbolic and psychological dimensions, connects the auditory experience to cultural practices and ancient traditions, and even proposes a practical challenge to engage with the sound of coins for personal enrichment. This multi-faceted approach aims to provide a comprehensive understanding of the role of coin cadence in shaping our perceptions and experiences of wealth.

Chapter 8

Vibrations of Value: Psychological Aspects of Money

Money as a Symbol of Worth and Self-Identity

The journey into understanding the frequency of money goes beyond the tangible exchange of bills and coins. Chapter 7 delves into the psychological dimensions of wealth, exploring how money serves as a powerful symbol of personal worth and self-identity. Just as vibrations shape our reality, the frequencies of beliefs and emotions surrounding money mold our financial experiences.

The Symbolic Resonance of Money

Money isn't merely a tool for transactions; it's a symbol that carries layers of meaning. It represents not only our purchasing power but also our status, security, and success. This chapter invites us to consider how our self-worth can become entwined with our financial worth, creating a complex interplay of frequencies that influence our choices, decisions, and behaviors.

As we assign value to money, we assign value to ourselves. The quest for financial abundance often becomes intertwined with the quest for personal validation, a pursuit that echoes in the frequencies of our thoughts and emotions. Just as music conveys emotions through melody and rhythm, our relationship with money is a symphony of feelings that can shape our financial outcomes.

Ameca Cooley

The Frequencies of Beliefs and Emotions Around Money

Our beliefs about money, often formed in childhood and influenced by societal norms, create frequencies that resonate within our subconscious. Positive beliefs can uplift our financial experiences, while negative beliefs can create energetic barriers to wealth. Likewise, emotions tied to money, guilt, excitement, or gratitude produce vibrations that ripple through our financial choices.

Exploring the frequencies of beliefs and emotions helps us uncover the undercurrents that shape our financial reality. For instance, if you believe that money is scarce, this belief creates a vibrational barrier to abundance. Conversely, if you cultivate a belief in the abundance of opportunities, you align yourself with frequencies that attract prosperity.

As we navigate the psychological dimensions of wealth, we'll uncover the techniques to reprogram limiting beliefs and transform emotional frequencies. By consciously reshaping our vibrational relationship with money, we can harmonize our thoughts and emotions to create a resonance that attracts financial success.

Through stories, exercises, and practical insights, this chapter guides you to recognize and understand the vibrational frequencies that stem from your beliefs and emotions about money. By aligning your internal frequencies with those of abundance, you'll embark on a transformational journey that elevates your financial reality and paves the way for a harmonious relationship with wealth.

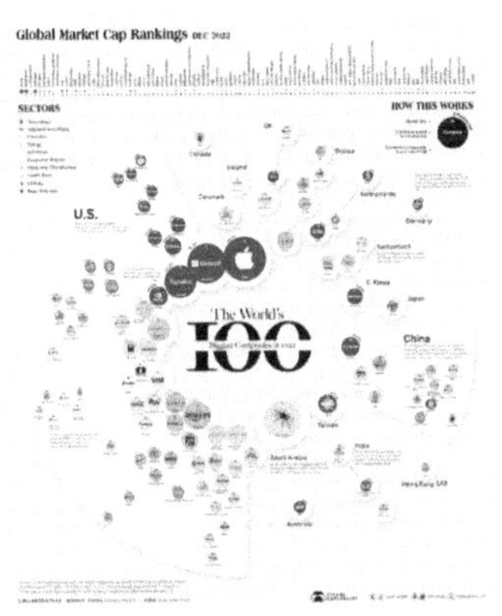

Chapter 9

Cultural Perspectives

Money's Frequency Across Cultures

In a globalized world, money's resonance extends far beyond its physical form. Chapter 8 explores the fascinating tapestry of cultural perspectives on money and how different societies assign value, significance, and meaning to currency. Just as frequencies of sound vary in different musical genres, the frequencies of money are modulated by cultural contexts.

Cultural norms, traditions, and historical contexts contribute to the unique frequencies associated with money in each culture. This chapter invites you to journey through diverse financial landscapes, shedding light on how money's vibrational essence reflects and shapes cultural identity. From communal values to individual aspirations, the frequency of money is a mirror reflecting the soul of societies.

Superstitions and Rituals Involving Money

Just as rituals and ceremonies use vibrations to create shared experiences, cultural practices around money carry their own vibrational resonance. This section delves into the superstitions, rituals, and taboos that cultures attach to money. From auspicious days for financial transactions to the belief in lucky charms, these practices reveal the intricate dance between money and metaphysics.

Whether it's the sound of coins clinking in a traditional ceremony or the act of giving "lucky money," these practices are more than symbolic gestures. They create frequencies that align with cultural values and beliefs, further connecting individuals to the vibrational currents of wealth and abundance.

Chapter 10

The Frequency of Giving

Philanthropy and Generosity

Chapter 10 takes us into the transformative frequencies of giving and how acts of generosity create a vibrational harmony that resonates not only with the giver and receiver, but also with God.

Just as harmonies emerge when musical notes are played together, the frequencies of giving create a beautiful resonance that amplifies positive energy.

Philanthropy and generosity transcend material transactions. They embody the spirit of abundance by channeling resources towards positive change. This section explores how individuals, companies, and communities align their frequencies with the act of giving, creating a harmonious symphony of shared prosperity.

How Acts of Giving Impact Financial Frequencies

The frequencies generated by giving are profound energies of compassion, empathy, and selflessness that reverberate across time and space. When you give without expectation, you align your frequency with the flow of abundance, creating a vibrational shift that can attract more prosperity into your life.

From the frequencies generated by donating to charitable causes to the vibrations of volunteer work, every act of giving contributes to the symphony of wealth creation. This section uncovers the ripple effects of giving, showing how the frequencies of generosity create a positive feedback loop that enhances financial well-being and amplifies the frequency of abundance.

By exploring the cultural perspectives of money and the frequency of giving, these chapters unveil the interconnectedness of wealth, society, and individual actions. As you journey through these pages, you'll discover the harmonious frequencies that underlie cultural practices and giving behaviors, allowing you to resonate with the higher frequencies of prosperity and positive change.

I had a situation yesterday with a woman on one of the teams that is a taker because she pretends to be a giver yet she will steal or try to unhand you any way she can. I sold her an expensive item at a cheap price. I also gave her some items I couldn't travel with, so she decided to charge me gas money afterward to get the money back for the item I sold her. This woman brought me credit clients to disturb my peace while gossiping about me to them. I shut her down from gossiping about them to me. One of the ladies told me what she was doing. Her daughter told me she went through my things at her home. I began to separate myself because she is low vibrating and is a false prophet that can only go so far. This woman is bound by the pretentiousness of her imagination. If she knew God's power within, she wouldn't have to steal or pretend. I manifest with words, movement, and thought. When I walk in rooms, lights flicker, things vibrate and water turns on because my presence is so strong. When I tell money to come, after I purpose money obeys me. When I tell a storm to stop, it obeys. I operate in the dominion given to me by the God that lives in me and has made me a God in this earth. Gen. 1 Verses 26 to 31

[28] And God blessed them, and God said unto them, Be fruitful, and multiply, and replenish the earth, and subdue it: and have dominion over the fish of the sea, and over the fowl of the air, and over every living thing that moveth upon the earth. I tell animals what to do and when I show up they come visit me. Vanity singer Prince's ex-girlfriend told me she shared the same ability with animals before she died. To see some of these videos click this link https://vimeo.com/863650569

Transforming Your Money Frequency: Healing Negative Beliefs

Identifying and Overcoming Limiting Beliefs About Money

In this transformative chapter, we delve deep into the realm of healing negative beliefs around money. Just as dissonant notes can be transformed into harmonies, the frequencies of your thoughts can be shifted to resonate with abundance. This section guides you through the process of recognizing and releasing limiting beliefs that hold you back from financial success.

"Do not be conformed to this world, but be transformed by the renewal of your mind." Romans 12:2*

Utilizing Sound, Meditation, and Affirmations for Transformation

Sound has the power to realign frequencies, and the sounds of your thoughts are no exception. Through meditation and affirmations, you can rewire your brain's vibrational patterns to align with prosperity. This chapter explores how mindfulness and intentional affirmation practices can reshape your beliefs and ultimately elevate your financial frequency.

In this concluding chapter, we embark on a transformative journey to heal negative beliefs about money, recognizing that just as dissonant notes can be transformed into harmonies, the frequencies of our thoughts can be shifted to resonate with abundance. The overarching theme is the renewal of the mind, drawing inspiration from Romans 12:2.

1. Transformation of Beliefs:

The central focus of the chapter is on identifying and overcoming limiting beliefs about money. The analogy of transforming dissonant notes into harmonies implies that even deeply ingrained negative beliefs can be reshaped for a more positive and harmonious financial mindset.

2. Guidance for Recognizing Limiting Beliefs:

The section promises to guide readers through the process of recognizing and releasing limiting beliefs that may be hindering their financial success. This acknowledgment of the need for inner transformation sets the stage for personal growth.

3. Biblical Wisdom:

Drawing wisdom from the Bible, particularly Romans 12:2, emphasizes the importance of not conforming to the world's limiting views but rather undergoing a transformative renewal of the mind. This biblical reference adds a spiritual dimension to the process of changing one's beliefs about money.

4. Utilizing Sound, Meditation, and Affirmations:

The chapter introduces the powerful tools of sound, meditation, and affirmations for transformation. The idea that sound has the ability to realign frequencies extends to the sounds of one's thoughts. Meditation and affirmations are presented as practical ways to rewire the brain's vibrational patterns, aligning them with the energy of prosperity.

5. Mindfulness and Affirmation Practices:

The exploration of mindfulness and intentional affirmation practices suggests a holistic approach to reshaping beliefs. By bringing awareness to thought patterns and actively affirming positive beliefs, individuals can work towards elevating their financial frequency.

6. Biblical Reference to Thought Power:

Quoting Proverbs 23:7, "As a man thinketh in his heart, so is he," reinforces the idea that our thoughts shape our reality. This biblical reference underscores the profound impact of thought patterns on one's identity and experiences.

7. Elevation of Financial Frequencies:

The ultimate goal is to elevate financial frequency. This implies a positive shift in the energy surrounding money, aligning with the principles of abundance and prosperity.

8. Renewal of the Mind:

The chapter's conclusion emphasizes the renewal of the mind as a transformative process. This aligns with the overarching theme of the book, highlighting the importance of changing one's mindset to attract financial success.

In conclusion, Chapter 11 serves as a guide to transforming your money frequency by healing negative beliefs. It integrates biblical wisdom, practical tools like sound, meditation, and affirmations, and emphasizes the power of thought in shaping one's financial reality. The journey toward a renewed and harmonious mindset is not just about wealth but about personal growth and well-being.

"As a man thinketh in his heart, so is he." Proverbs 23:7*

Chapter 12

Giving and Receiving: Frequencies of Generosity

Exploring the Vibrational Dynamics of Giving

Chapter 12 leads us into the harmonious dance between giving and receiving a symphony that has reverberated through centuries. Just as musical harmonies blend to create a beautiful composition, the frequencies of generosity create a harmonious resonance that nurtures both giver and receiver. This section takes you on a journey through the spiritual and vibrational dimensions of giving.

"Give, and it will be given to you. A good measure, pressed down, shaken together and running over, will be poured into your lap." Luke 6:38

How Acts of Generosity Impact Wealth's Frequencies

The frequencies emitted by acts of generosity are of unparalleled potency. This section explores how the intention behind your giving creates a resonance that echoes far beyond the act itself. When you give with an open heart and a frequency of abundance, you attune yourself to the frequencies of prosperity, inviting more abundance into your life.

It is more blessed to give than to receive." Acts 20:35

Chapter 13

Currency in Culture: Vibrations Across Different Societies

Examining Cultural Perspectives on Wealth and Currency

In this chapter, we embark on a cross-cultural journey, exploring how different societies and traditions infuse unique frequencies into the realm of wealth and currency. Like the harmonies in a global orchestra, these perspectives create a rich symphony of beliefs and practices that shape financial experiences worldwide.

As we delve into the diverse cultural tapestry, we discover that the concept of wealth extends far beyond the mere accumulation of currency. It intertwines with deep-rooted values, historical narratives, and spiritual beliefs, resonating through generations. From ancient wisdom to modern practices, each culture contributes distinctive notes to the melody of financial understanding.

One notable aspect we explore is the symbiotic relationship between an individual's beliefs and their financial reality. The quote from Matthew 6:21 serves as a guiding light: *"For where your treasure is, there your heart will be also."* This timeless wisdom encourages reflection on the profound connection between one's values and the pursuit of wealth. From the bustling markets of Asia to the corporate boardrooms of the West, this principle echoes, reminding us that our financial pursuits are often intertwined with the matters of the heart and soul.

Throughout this chapter, we'll navigate through cultural landscapes that assign diverse meanings to wealth. Whether it's the communal values of certain African societies, the ascetic traditions of Eastern philosophies, or the materialistic ethos of some Western cultures, each perspective casts a unique resonance on the tapestry of global financial cultures.

In doing so, we'll contemplate questions that delve into the heart of cultural perceptions: What is the purpose of wealth in different societies? How do cultural values influence economic practices? How do various communities define prosperity, and what rituals or practices mark significant financial milestones?

As we uncover these cultural vibrations, it becomes apparent that the concept of currency extends far beyond paper notes and digital transactions. It becomes a carrier of cultural identity, a transmitter of shared values, and a testament to the diverse ways humanity approaches the intricate dance between material wealth and spiritual richness.

Join us on this exploration as we listen to the echoes of wisdom from cultures around the world, discovering how these vibrations shape the dynamic relationship between individuals, societies, and the universal pursuit of prosperity.

In this chapter, we embark on a cross-cultural journey, exploring how different societies and traditions infuse unique frequencies into the realm of wealth and currency. Like the harmonies in a global orchestra, these perspectives create a rich symphony of beliefs and practices that shape financial experiences worldwide.

Your life Purpose has a monetary frequency

Your purpose in life carries a monetary frequency that extends beyond mere financial gain. It encompasses the idea that aligning your endeavors with your true calling can lead to not only personal fulfillment but also prosperity in various aspects of life, including financial well-being. When you discover and pursue your purpose with passion and dedication, you emit a unique vibrational energy that attracts opportunities, abundance, and success. It suggests that the pursuit of your life's purpose can bring about a harmonious alignment with the universe, allowing you to tap into resources and avenues that contribute to both your personal and financial growth. This perspective encourages a holistic approach, emphasizing the interconnectedness of purpose, abundance, and a fulfilling life journey.

"Whoever loves money never has enough; whoever loves wealth is never satisfied with their income." Ecclesiastes 5:10

Through these chapters, you'll explore the profound connections between beliefs, practices, and frequencies, discovering how aligning your thoughts, actions, and intentions can harmonize with the frequencies of abundance and transform your financial reality.

Just as composers envision the future of music, financial experts predict the harmonious shifts that technological advancements will bring. This section offers insights into the potential vibrational changes in the financial world, highlighting how the frequency of money may transform with the rise of artificial intelligence, decentralized finance, and more.

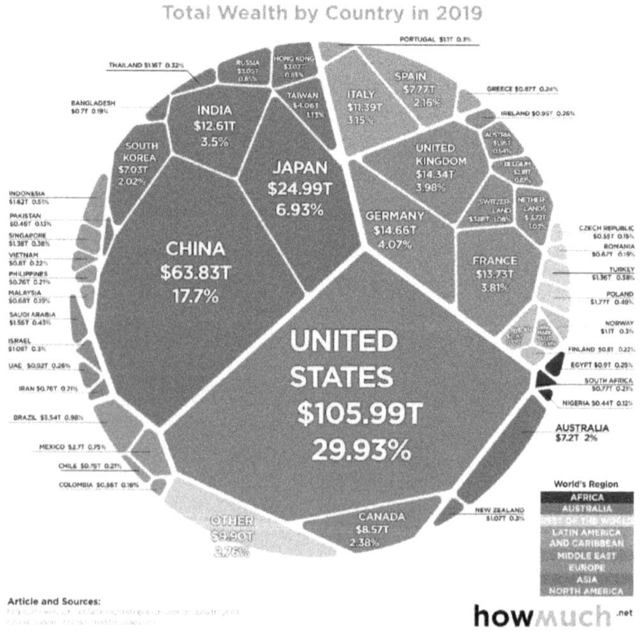

Chapter 14

The Future Symphony: Technological Advancements in Currency

Technological Innovations and Their Effects on Money's Frequencies

This chapter invites us on a prophetic journey into the evolving landscape of currency, drawing parallels between the advancing world of music and the transformative forces shaping the financial realm. Just as musicians explore new instruments and techniques, the symphony of finance is orchestrated by technological innovations. In this exploration, we delve into the vibrational frequencies of digital currencies, blockchain technology, and the profound impact of fintech on the financial symphony.

"Behold, I am making all things new." - Revelation 21:5

The biblical verse from Revelation 21:5 serves as a guiding light, echoing the divine promise of renewal. As we navigate through the unprecedented technological advancements, we witness a renaissance in the financial landscape, a rebirth marked by the advent of new instruments and the harmonization of novel financial frequencies.

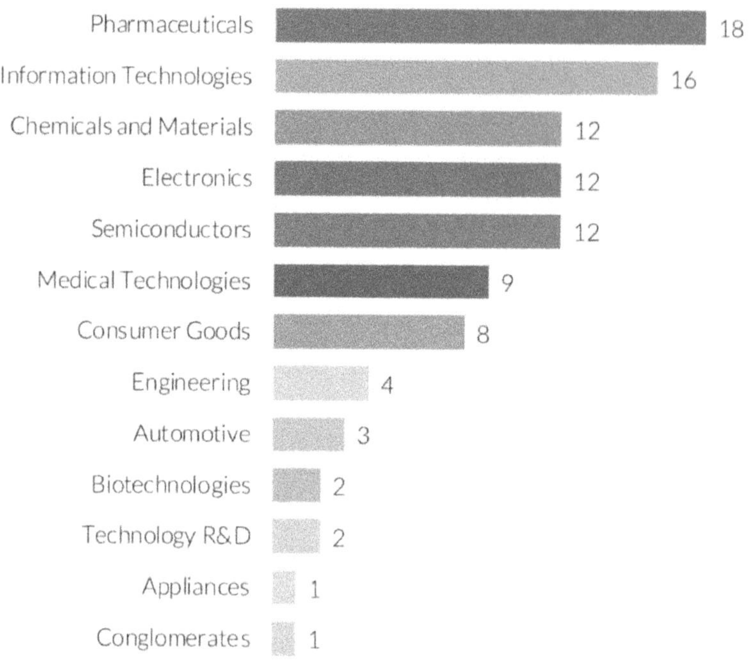

Predictions for the Future of Financial Vibrations

Much like composers envision the future of music, financial experts endeavor to predict the harmonious shifts that technological advancements will bring. This section offers scripturally-informed insights into the potential vibrational changes in the financial world, highlighting how the frequency of money may transform with the rise of artificial intelligence, decentralized finance, and more.

Proverbs 16:9 (NIV): "In their hearts, humans plan their course, but the Lord establishes their steps."

As humanity plans the course of financial evolution through technological innovations, the divine guidance of the Lord establishes the steps, ensuring that these advancements align with principles of justice, fairness, and ethical considerations.

The financial symphony of the future introduces digital currencies as key players, their frequencies resonating in the decentralized realms of blockchain technology. Cryptocurrencies, with their promises of security, transparency, and efficiency, become integral notes in the composition of this evolving financial opus.

Isaiah 43:19 (NIV): "See, I am doing a new thing! Now it springs up; do you not perceive it? I am making a way in the wilderness and streams in the wasteland."

The rise of fintech, akin to a groundbreaking composition, introduces new rhythms and beats to the traditional financial arrangement. Artificial intelligence in financial management becomes an avant-garde movement, challenging conventional practices and introducing innovative ways of conducting monetary transactions.

As we contemplate decentralized finance, *Galatians 3:28 (NIV)* reminds us: "There is neither Jew nor Gentile, neither slave nor free, nor is there male and female, for you are all one in Christ Jesus." Similarly, decentralized finance disperses once-centralized notes of financial authority, creating a more democratic and interconnected financial score.

This chapter explores not only the technological advancements but also the ethical and societal implications they bring. The harmonic evolution of financial frequencies should resonate not only with efficiency but also with principles of fairness, security, and accessibility.

In the chapters ahead, we will continue to explore the unfolding symphony of financial technologies, contemplating their melodies and harmonies. The journey into the future of financial vibrations promises to be both captivating and transformative, echoing the scriptural assurance that, indeed, all things are being made new.

"But let justice roll down like waters, and righteousness like an ever-flowing stream." Amos 5:24

Chapter 15

Prosperity Mindset in Practice: Practical Exercises

Meditation and Visualization Techniques for Financial Harmony

Chapter 14 provides practical tools to harmonize your financial frequencies through meditation and visualization. Just as musicians rehearse to perfect their performance, you can practice techniques that align your thoughts and emotions with abundance. This section guides you through mindful practices that attune you to the frequency of prosperity.

"Whatever you ask in prayer, believe that you have received it, and it will be yours." Mark 11:24

Crafting Personal Rituals to Align with Abundance

Similar to musicians incorporating rituals before a performance, you can create personal rituals that amplify your vibrational connection to wealth. This section explores the creation of routines and practices that align with the frequency of prosperity, infusing your daily life with harmonious financial energy.

"Let the favor of the Lord our God be upon us, and establish the work of our hands upon us; yes, establish the work of our hands!" Psalm 90:17

My ritual

Pray

Read these scriptures

Sure, here are 33 Bible verses that touch on the themes of wealth and abundance:

1. Deuteronomy 8:18 (NIV):

But remember the Lord your God, for it is he who gives you the ability to produce wealth.

2. Proverbs 3:9-10 (NIV):

Honor the Lord with your wealth, with the firstfruits of all your crops; then your barns will be filled to overflowing, and your vats will brim over with new wine.

3. Malachi 3:10 (NIV):

Bring the whole tithe into the storehouse, that there may be food in my house. Test me in this," says the Lord Almighty, "and see if I will not throw open the floodgates of heaven and pour out so much blessing that there will not be room enough to store it.

4. Psalm 37:4 (NIV):

Take delight in the Lord, and he will give you the desires of your heart.

5. Matthew 6:33 (NIV):

But seek first his kingdom and his righteousness, and all these things will be given to you as well.

6. Proverbs 22:4 (NIV):

Humility is the fear of the Lord; its wages are riches and honor and life.

7. Ecclesiastes 5:19 (NIV):

Moreover, when God gives someone wealth and possessions, and the ability to enjoy them, to accept their lot and be happy in their toil—this is a gift of God.

8. Proverbs 10:22 (NIV):

The blessing of the Lord brings wealth, without painful toil for it.

9. Philippians 4:19 (NIV):

And my God will meet all your needs according to the riches of his glory in Christ Jesus.

10. Proverbs 13:11 (NIV):

Dishonest money dwindles away, but whoever gathers money little by little makes it grow.

11. Luke 6:38 (NIV):

Give, and it will be given to you. A good measure, pressed down, shaken together and running over, will be poured into your lap. For with the measure you use, it will be measured to you.

12. 1 Timothy 6:17 (NIV):

Command those who are rich in this present world not to be arrogant nor to put their hope in wealth, which is so uncertain, but to put their hope in God, who richly provides us with everything for our enjoyment.

13. Proverbs 28:25 (NIV):

The greedy stir up conflict, but those who trust in the Lord will prosper.

14. Haggai 2:8 (NIV):

'The silver is mine and the gold is mine,' declares the Lord Almighty.

15. Matthew 19:26 (NIV):

Yeshua looked at them and said, "With man this is impossible, but with God all things are possible."

16. Psalm 112:1-3 (NIV):

Praise the Lord. Blessed are those who fear the Lord, who find great delight in his commands. Their children will be mighty in the land; the generation of the upright will be blessed. Wealth and riches are in their houses, and their righteousness endures forever.

17. 2 Corinthians 9:8 (NIV):

And God is able to bless you abundantly, so that in all things at all times, having all that you need, you will abound in every good work.

18. Proverbs 3:16 (NIV):

Long life is in her right hand; in her left hand are riches and honor.

19. Ecclesiastes 3:13 (NIV):

That each of them may eat and drink, and find satisfaction in all their toil—this is the gift of God.

20. Psalm 23:1 (NIV):

The Lord is my shepherd, I lack nothing.

21. Proverbs 11:25 (NIV):

A generous person will prosper; whoever refreshes others will be refreshed.

22. 1 Chronicles 29:12 (NIV):

Wealth and honor come from you; you are the ruler of all things. In your hands are strength and power to exalt and give strength to all.

23. Proverbs 14:23 (NIV):

All hard work brings a profit, but mere talk leads only to poverty.

24. Psalm 1:3 (NIV):

That person is like a tree planted by streams of water, which yields its fruit in season and whose leaf does not wither—whatever they do prospers.

25. 1 Timothy 6:10 (NIV):

For the love of money is a root of all kinds of evil. Some people, eager for money, have wandered from the faith and pierced themselves with many griefs.

26. Proverbs 8:18 (NIV):

With me are riches and honor, enduring wealth and prosperity.

27. Luke 12:15 (NIV):

Then he said to them, "Watch out! Be on your guard against all kinds of greed; life does not consist in an abundance of possessions."

28. Proverbs 28:20 (NIV):

A faithful person will be richly blessed, but one eager to get rich will not go unpunished.

29. Psalm 84:11 (NIV):

For the Lord God is a sun and shield; the Lord bestows favor and honor; no good thing does he withhold from those whose walk is blameless.

30. Matthew 6:19-21 (NIV):

Do not store up for yourselves treasures on earth, where moths and vermin destroy, and where thieves break in and steal. But store up for yourselves treasures in heaven, where moths and vermin do not destroy, and where thieves do not break in and steal. For where your treasure is, there your heart will be also.

31. Psalm 37:25 (NIV):

I was young and now I am old, yet I have never seen the righteous forsaken or their children begging bread.

32. Proverbs 3:13-16 (NIV):

Blessed are those who find wisdom, those who gain understanding, for she is more profitable than silver and yields better returns than gold. She is more precious than rubies; nothing you desire can compare with her. Long life is in her right hand; in her left hand are riches and honor.

33. Jeremiah 29:11 (NIV):

For I know the plans I have for you, declares the Lord, plans for welfare and not for evil, to give you a future and a hope.

Listen to promises of God which is my voice making suggestions to my brain.

Listen to plannetimv.com 8 am to 8:30am while in the shower or bath

Mary Kay beauty regimen 1. Skincare 2. Makeup 3. Sun-care 4. Perfume Here is the link with my system Click to start your regimen now. https://www.marykay.com/msameca/en-us/ products?iad=topnavpws_ shop when you look good you feel good and that increases your vibrations and frequency.

Listen to money sounds and frequencies while eating breakfast https:// youtube.com/@nowinvestmentsinc5217?si=z-UEhb3cT0VMUJbQ

Monday I set my goals , run errands, Monday and Wednesday teach others to generate wealth click here to join now

https://feee-inc.trainercentralsite.com/course/feeeinc?email-Id=zsa%40zsazsagroup.com#/course/3291948000000013009/attend/section/3291948000000051011/lesson/3291948000000066065

Tuesday through Friday, help my team and make calls for our businesses 10 am to 7 pm in 15 min intervals, while my staff work.

Saturday I rest spend time meditating, praying and Going to events after sunset

Sunday I teach online finance classes.

Travel and enjoy life

Sundays call family and friends, metaphysical healing sessions 12. Read books until I fall asleep

Last night, God showed me in a dream how all of my prayers had been answered. I desired residual income and I have it from several sources. I desire to go to spas all over the world and my travel business allows me to do that. To learn more, click this link now

https://tap.bio/@GEfFMW7TNMIaEVpAfqeARKnoIJY9wLpuibzFU-NIq9xdqkmhmg_aem_ AeIxaD6QruTJO8b7Y91A5gYTxXNpwN-hq2_7GasM-0yCRdLO64jsBPP60PVstffbLPqA

Closing Notes: Harmonious Abundance

Recapitulating the Frequencies of Money

As a symphony concludes with a recapitulation, this chapter revisits the key frequencies explored throughout the book. It reinforces the understanding that just as harmonies in music create a complete composition, the harmonies of financial frequencies contribute to a fulfilling and abundant life.

"I came that they may have life and have it abundantly. "
John 10:10

Embracing a Mindset of Harmonious Wealth

In the final notes of this journey, Chapter 15 invites you to embrace a mindset of harmonious wealth. Just as music lingers in our ears, the frequencies of prosperity can resonate within you. This section encourages you to carry forward the lessons learned and align your thoughts, actions, and intentions with the frequencies of abundance.

"For as he thinks in his heart, so is he." Proverbs 23:7

This comprehensive outline covers the various aspects you mentioned, while offering insights, analysis, practical exercises, and connections to biblical scriptures. Each chapter delves deep into its topic, providing a comprehensive exploration of the frequency of money and prosperity.

To clear your mind, pray first, meditate second, eat healthily afterward.

Here's a list of 33 high-frequency foods that are commonly recognized for their nutritional value and health benefits:

- **Spinach**
- **Kale**
- **Broccoli**
- **Sweet potatoes**
- **Avocado**
- **Blueberries**
- **Strawberries**
- **Plums**
- **Quinoa**
- **Oats**
- **Almonds**
- **Walnuts**
- **Chia seeds**
- **Flaxseeds**
- **Pineapples**
- **Maitake Mushrooms**
- **Acai**
- **Lentils**
- **Brown rice**
- **Tomatoes**

- **Oranges**
- **Apples**
- **Carrots**
- **Bell peppers**
- **Cucumbers**
- **Garlic**
- **Ginger**
- **Turmeric**
- **Olive oil**
- **Green tea**
- **Watermelon**
- **Cabbage**
- **Pomegranate**

These foods are packed with essential nutrients, antioxidants, and health-promoting properties, making them a great addition to a balanced diet.

Cleanse and get rid of toxins and parasites. Use this link for products https://shop.totallifechanges.com/home?lang=en&sponsor=Acooley

Chapter 17

Proximity to High Billionaire Frequency: Elevating Your Income

Understanding the Power of Proximity

In the world of wealth creation, there's a phenomenon that goes beyond traditional strategies and financial planning. Chapter 16 takes us on a journey into the concept of proximity to high billionaire frequency, an idea that suggests that being in the vicinity of those who exude a billionaire mindset can impact your income and financial success.

The Vibrational Influence of High Billionaire Frequency

Much like how our personal frequencies impact our experiences, the frequencies emitted by individuals with immense wealth and success can influence those around them. This chapter explores the notion that these successful individuals, often referred to as "high billionaires," emit an energetic frequency that resonates with abundance, opportunity, and prosperity.

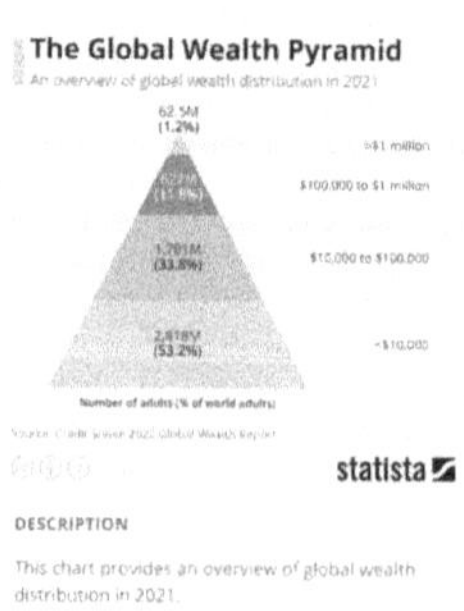

Ripple Effects on Income

Being in close proximity to those who operate on a high billionaire frequency can create a ripple effect on your financial outcomes. This doesn't just involve physical proximity, it can also encompass exposure to their thoughts, actions, and ways of thinking. Just as tuning forks resonate when placed near a vibrating object, aligning yourself with individuals who are in harmony with success can elevate your own vibrational frequency.

Learning From High Billionaire Frequency

The chapter delves into the strategies and mindsets that high billionaires often embody. By observing their habits, decision-making processes, and approaches to wealth creation, you can gain valuable insights that transcend traditional financial advice. Surrounding yourself with those who have mastered the art of financial growth provides a living example of the principles and behaviors that resonate with prosperity.

Creating Your Circle of Influence

Building a network of like-minded individuals who vibrate at a high frequency is a strategic move in cultivating financial success. This chapter offers practical steps to help you connect with individuals who align with your aspirations and who can help elevate your financial journey. From mentorship to collaboration, your circle of influence can propel you towards vibrational alignment with wealth.

By understanding the dynamics of proximity to high billionaire frequency, you can tap into an often unspoken aspect of financial success. Through this exploration, you'll gain insights into how vibrational alignment with abundance can impact your income, creating a harmonious resonance that elevates your financial path.

My income decreased when I spent too much time around and speaking with people who lived in poverty, that were takers, and were low vibrational. When I got in the room with Millionaires and Billionaires I began to shed off old relationships that couldn't go past the capacity of 6 figures. It is ok to reach back for those reaching forward but not for zombies. I used to say I am climbing a mountain, but I can't carry you because you are to heavy so that would cause us both to fall. Let go of poverty thoughts now. Let go of that man or woman that doesn't want you now. Let go of anyone who abuses you or your relationship now. Stop playing nice with satan. Let go of fear now. Wake up and live your dream life now. Throw those old clothes away. Stop horsing now. Stop lying so people don't lie to you. Start your skincare routine and beauty affirmations now. How write a strategy or email me now for a strategy session info@feeeinc.com .

So as a man thinketh in his heart so is he.

The frequency of thought, in terms of brain activity, is typically measured in Hertz (Hz), which represents the number of oscillations or cycles per second. Brain activity involves a wide range of frequencies, including delta, theta, alpha, beta, and gamma waves, each associated with different cognitive states. The specific frequency of thought can vary depending on the mental task or state a person is experiencing.

If you have read any of my other books, you know I always share affirmations that work.

Here is the affirmation for this book.

"I am not just a gate opener; I am a wealth of abundance, a vessel of charity, a beacon of love, a fountain of happiness, a harbinger of success, a channel for power and dominion, and a sacred temple of God on this earth. Money flows through me effortlessly, and I attract prosperity in all aspects of my life. I am attuned to the frequency of abundance, and my actions align with the symphony of wealth. I am a wise steward of my resources, and I use them to create positive vibrations in the world. I am a magnet for financial success, and opportunities to increase my wealth manifest abundantly. I am grateful for the blessings of abundance, and I share my prosperity generously. I am in harmony with the universal energies of prosperity, and I am a co-creator of my financial destiny. So be it. "Earth. #Affirmation #Abundance #Purpose"

Wealth Meditation

Wealth allows you to come and go anywhere in the world any time you please. Nothing has you bound. Eat what you want, wear what you want, and say what you want. My life is a reflection of who God is in my life . My beauty, my house, my car, my marriage, my children, my friends, my income, my investments, my partnerships, my words, my thoughts, my love, my philanthropy, and all of my being.

Homework

Listen to money sounds 3 times per day with money in your hand. https://youtube.com/@nowinvestmentsinc5217?si=z-UEhb3cT0VMU-JbQ

Write a review on how this book changed your financial life. Thank you in advance The Money Doctor and Metaphysist Ameca Cooley

Universal Law

The Bible contains principles that are often considered universal, applicable across cultures and time periods. Here are some key principles that many people view as universal laws based on biblical teachings:

1. Love your neighbor as yourself (Matthew 22:39):

"Love your neighbor as yourself" is a commandment that emphasizes the importance of showing love, compassion, and kindness to others.

2. The Golden Rule (Matthew 7:12):

"So in everything, do to others what you would have them do to you" encourages treating others with the same respect and kindness you would like to receive.

3. Forgiveness (Matthew 6:14-15):

"For if you forgive other people when they sin against you, your heavenly Father will also forgive you. But if you do not forgive others their sins, your Father will not forgive your sins." Forgiveness is a universal principle that promotes emotional and spiritual well-being.

4. Humility (Philippians 2:3-4):

"Do nothing out of selfish ambition or vain conceit. Rather, in humility value others above yourselves, not looking to your own interests but each of you to the interests of the others." Humility is a virtue that fosters healthy relationships and community.

5. Justice and Fairness (Micah 6:8):

"He has shown you, O mortal, what is good. And what does the Lord require of you? To act justly and to love mercy and to walk humbly with your God." This verse emphasizes the importance of justice, mercy, and humility.

6. Stewardship (Genesis 2:15):

"The Lord God took the man and put him in the Garden of Eden to work it and take care of it." This verse speaks to the concept of responsible stewardship of the environment and resources.

7. Seeking Wisdom (Proverbs 4:7):

"The beginning of wisdom is this: Get wisdom. Though it cost all you have, get understanding." Seeking wisdom is a universal principle that guides decision-making and actions.

8. Faith (Hebrews 11:1):

"Now faith is confidence in what we hope for and assurance about what we do not see." Faith is often seen as a universal principle that provides strength, hope, and perseverance.

9. Gratitude (1 Thessalonians 5:16-18):

"Rejoice always, pray continually, give thanks in all circumstances; for this is God's will for you in Christ Jesus." Gratitude is a universal principle that promotes a positive mindset and contentment.

10. Generosity (2 Corinthians 9:7):

"Each of you should give what you have decided in your heart to give, not reluctantly or under compulsion, for God loves a cheerful giver." Generosity is a principle that emphasizes selfless giving and sharing.

11. Unity (Ephesians 4:3):

"Make every effort to keep the unity of the Spirit through the bond of peace." This verse encourages believers to work towards unity and harmony.

12. Integrity (Proverbs 10:9):

"Whoever walks in integrity walks securely, but whoever takes crooked paths will be found out." Integrity is a universal principle that emphasizes honesty and moral uprightness.

These principles are often considered timeless and applicable to people of various cultural, religious, and philosophical backgrounds. They provide guidance for ethical living and positive relationships.

Use these scriptures to take authority over what belongs to you,

1. Binding the forces of darkness:

Ephesians 6:12 (NIV):* "For our struggle is not against flesh and blood, but against the rulers, against the authorities, against the powers of this dark world and against the spiritual forces of evil in the heavenly realms."

2. No weapon formed against us shall prosper:

Isaiah 54:17 (NIV):* "No weapon forged against you will prevail, and you will refute every tongue that accuses you. This is the heritage of the servants of the Lord, and this is their vindication from me," declares the Lord.

3. Authority in the name of Jesus:

Philippians 2:9-10 (NIV):* "Therefore God exalted him to the highest place and gave him the name that is above every name, that at the name of Yeshua every knee should bow, in heaven and on earth and under the earth."

4. Angels encamping around us:

Psalm 34:7 (NIV):* "The angel of the Lord encamps around those who fear him, and he delivers them."

5. Releasing prosperity:

3 John 1:2 (NIV):* "Dear friend, I pray that you may enjoy good

health and that all may go well with you, even as your soul is getting along well."

6. More than conquerors through Christ:

Romans 8:37 (NIV):* "No, in all these things we are more than conquerors through him who loved us."

Chronicles 7:14 (NIV):

"If my people, who are called by my name, will humble themselves and pray and seek my face and turn from their wicked ways, then I will hear from heaven, and I will forgive their sin and will heal their land."

Feel free to incorporate these scriptures into your prayer or meditate on them as you seek the Lord's guidance and protection.

Heavenly Father,

In the name of Yeshua, we come before you with hearts filled with gratitude and reverence. We acknowledge Your sovereignty and authority over all things, and we stand on the promises of Your Word.

We declare that Yeshua the Messiah is Lord over our lives, and through His name, we bind up every force of darkness that seeks to steal, block, or hinder the good success and prosperity that You have intended for us.

We bind up satan, the accuser, and all his schemes. We declare that no weapon formed against us shall prosper, and every tongue that rises against us in judgment shall be condemned.

In the powerful name of Yeshua, we bind all principalities in high places, the prince of Persia, and every evil force that opposes your will God for our lives. We break every chain, every stronghold, and every assignment of the enemy.

We specifically bind the work of witches, demons, and warlocks, declaring that their plans are null and void in the face of Your mighty power. We cause any personal items, hair, blood, body fluids that have been stolen from use to be burned and destroyed. Every doll, paper, food, poop, or spell casting item with our picture or name on it may it be destroyed with fire. Deuteronomy 28:7 (NIV): "The Lord will grant that the enemies who rise up against you will be defeated before you. They will come at you from one direction but flee from you in seven." Exodus 22:18 (ESV), which states: "You shall not permit a sorceress to live."We command every evil spirit to flee at the sound of Your name.

Lord, we ask for Your protection and for a hedge of angels to surround us, guarding us against every attack. Your Word says that the angel of the Lord encamps around those who fear Him and delivers them.

We now loose, in the name of Yeshua, all the good success that You have intended for us. We release prosperity in every area of our lives— spiritually, emotionally, physically, and financially. Your Word declares that we are more than conquerors through the Messiah who strengthens us.

We thank You, Lord, for Your faithfulness, and we receive by faith all the blessings and breakthroughs that You have in store for us. May Your will be done on earth as it is in heaven.

In Yeshua's mighty name, we pray.

Amen.

Yeshua the correct name not Jesus. satan had the Europeans create that name to deceive the world, removing the power out the name. They used the name to make the rest of the world identify Yeshua to be like them and to control other nations during slavery and colonization. This was so that the slaves wouldn't know who they were and would lose their identity. Willie Lynch said it would take a miracle to set them free. Thank you, God, for the Miracle of your word that has the power to free us and that gives us our true identity and purpose for our lives.

Hosea 4:6 (NIV), and it goes:"My people are destroyed from lack of knowledge. Because you have rejected knowledge, I also reject you as my priests; because you have ignored the law of your God, I also will ignore your children."

This verse emphasizes the importance of knowledge, particularly knowledge of God's laws and ways. It suggests that a lack of understanding and adherence to God's principles can lead to destruction and negative consequences. The rejection of knowledge and the ignoring of God's law are seen as serious matters, impacting not only individuals but also future generations.

It underscores the value of seeking wisdom and understanding, especially in matters of faith and righteous living. This theme resonates throughout the Bible, emphasizing the significance of a deep and intimate knowledge of God and His teachings for a prosperous and righteous life.

Do not be deceived satanic spirits and demons have to eat aborted babies and the blood of humans to live because God is not providing for them. You do not have to sell your soul if you read an do the Godly things in this book. When people do witchcraft and root work they do detestable things like eating feces, drinking blood and urine, sacrificing their family, incest, sexual crimes, and all matters of evil.

Satan is a master marketer, he has been repackaging & selling the same lie for centuries. Namely, "you can be happy w/o God." #liar

Satan say what would you like money, sex, women, cars, fame, confidence aka pride ? You will be given a satanic spirit to accomplish that aka your alter ego. He will be praised and glorified. You will eventually become a zombie and your family will be cursed generationally. God says I came that you may have life and life more abundantly. You will have wealth, wisdom, understanding, love, marriage, generational blessing. You will receive the Holy Spirit to help you to accomplish it. God gives full transparency on the conditions. satan reveals more after the ritual is complete and when the angel of death comes to collect your soul. satan hates humans because we are the image of God and God loves us so he will do anything to trick you into destroying yourself and others.

All spells and rituals require a sacrifice. God requires a sacrifice. All power comes from God. Proverbs 5:5 In-Context 3 For the lips of the adulterous woman drip honey, and her speech is smoother than oil; 4 but in the end she is bitter as gall, sharp as a double-edged sword. 5 Her feet go down to death; her steps lead straight to the grave. Exodus 22:18 Do not allow a sorceress to live. Thou shalt not suffer a witch to live.

Remember to forgive, love, and most importantly put God first. Matthew 6:33 (NIV):

"But seek first his kingdom and his righteousness, and all these things will be given to you as well."